On the Moon

Faridah Yusof

Table of Contents

Astronauts 4

The Sky 6

Air and Water 8

The Ground 10

Earth 12

moon

On Earth, we can see the **moon** in the sky.

Astronauts

Astronauts have gone to the **moon**.

They saw what the **moon** is like.

The Sky

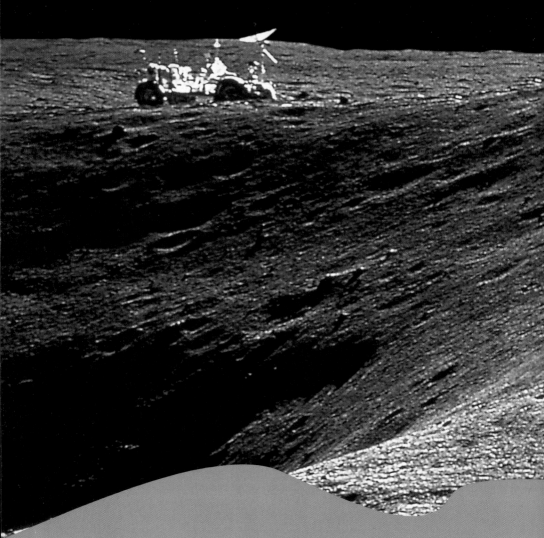

On the **moon**, the sky
is always dark and clear.

There are no clouds.

Air and Water

On the **moon**, there is no air
or water.

There is no wind.
Nothing lives on the **moon**.

The Ground

On the **moon**, the ground is rocky.

There are mountains and valleys.

Earth

Earth

On the **moon**, you can see Earth in the sky.

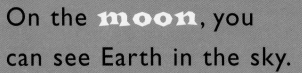

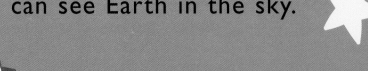